MW01228566

creepy little death poems

by
Tiffany Tang

Lizzie Silverman, Illustrator

Published in the United States of America by Dreality Press
11333 N. Moorpark Blvd #35
Studio City, CA 91602

Illustrations by Lizzie Silverman

Copyright © 2014 Tiffany Tang
All rights reserved.
ISBN-13: 978-0615961569 (Dreality Press)
ISBN-10: 0615961568
First Edition

For Christy and the wise ones who believe.

1.
Death.
We seem to understand each other better these days.
Maybe it's because I'm stalking him. I don't know.
I don't have malicious intentions.
I just want to know him better.
I ask him, "Hey, Death. What's up?"
Sometimes, we sit next to each other at Starbucks.
We don't say much, just sip our coffee and share space.
Sometimes, Death asks me,
"Why do you want to know me so badly?"
Sometimes, I answer, "I just want to try you on."
"How do I fit?" he asks.
"Too easily," I say.
"Well, that won't do," says Death.
"After all, you like things extra complicated."
It's true.
Death knows me well.
Finally, I say to Death, "Let's go home."

2.

I find Death in the bedroom where he is hanging curtains.

"Death," I ask. "What do you think of Christmas music?"

Death doesn't stop what he is doing, but he looks over his shoulder and watches me, my head bowed in concentration, scrolling through my iTunes playlists.

"I like Christmas," Death says.

He goes back to hanging the curtains.

"But what about the music?" I persist, looking up at him.

Death stops hanging the curtains. He turns around.

"Why are you asking me about Christmas?"

He is stern.

"I just want to know," I reply.

"Do *you* like Christmas music?" he asks.

"Yes," I say.

"Then why am *I* here?" Death asks.

I stare at Death for a moment and then I leave the room, cheeks burning.

Shut up, Death, I think. *What do you know?*

3.

Death casually pops his head around the corner.

"Watcha doin'?" he asks.

"Baking cookies," I say.

Death watches me crack eggs into the mixer. One-handed.

"Do you...want to talk about it?" he asks.

"About what?" I say, measuring out the baking soda.

"About the fact that it's the middle of the night and you're cranking Josh Groban and baking cookies like your life depends on it," says Death.

I pause mid-chocolate chip pour.

"It doesn't, by the way," he says.

"What?" I ask.

"Depend on it," he clarifies. "Your life doesn't depend on it."

Death looks at me earnestly.

"Trust me," he says. "I know."

Death thinks he's funny.

I finish pouring the chocolate chips.

"Can I help?" he asks.

I eye him suspiciously.

"Do you even have hands?" I motion impatiently with my spatula towards the long black sleeves, which droop from his cloak and disappear into nothingness.

He follows my gaze.

"Oh," says Death. "Good point."

4.

"It's 11:11."

Death looks up at me from behind the newspaper.

"What?" he asks, lowering the travel section.

"It's 11:11," I say. "Make a wish."

Death closes his eyes for a moment. I do the same.

He opens them and goes back to the travel section.

I wait.

I watch him clumsily turn the pages of the newspaper.

"Well?" I ask, finally.

He looks up at me again.

"What?" he asks.

He's being deliberately obtuse.

"Well, what did you wish for?" I ask.

"I can't tell you that. It won't come true," says Death.

We stare at each other for a long moment.

Finally, I say, "You don't really believe that, do you?"

Death sighs.

"Of course not."

He begins to peruse an article about Bora Bora.

"But you do," says Death.

5.
"Stop it."
"No."
"Stop it."
"No."
"Stop it."
"No."
"Stop it."
"You," I say to Death, "stop being so bossy."
"You," Death says to me, "stop brooding.
Your aura is darker than mine."
I look up at him.
"Heh, heh, heh," says Death,
elbowing me like a Marx brother.
I get up from the sofa and head into the kitchen.
"Leave me alone," I say.
"Okay," says Death.
"But cookie-baking won't solve this problem."
I pause mid-step.
"Fine," I say, without turning around.
"Then you don't get any."
I continue into the kitchen.
"Who's bossy now?" Death calls from the living room.

6.

My mother wants to stop in and see my grandmother at her retirement home.

I ask if Death can come.

She looks at me, smiles awkwardly, and gets into the car.

I look at Death and shrug.

"That's okay," says Death. "You know how I hate that place. Everyone is always staring at me like I'm out to get them or something."

"Some people are just bigots, Death," I tell him.

"You can't take it personally."

Death nods. He goes into the house.

After a moment, I hear the sound of the television.

7.

"I can't believe it's opening night," I say.

Death is sewing the armbands for my costume.

Unwound spools of hot pink thread tangle in his dark, flowing robes of darkness.

"Don't be nervous," says Death, mid-sew.

"I'm not," I say. Then, I eye him suspiciously.

"Wait." I say. "Do you know something I don't?"

Death tilts his head to one side.

"Maybe," he says.

I swallow.

A long awkward moment ensues.

Death holds up a perfectly sewn armband for my perusal.

"What do you think?" he asks.

I am holding my breath.

Death looks at me.

"Oh, for Pete's sake," says Death.

"Learn how to take a joke."

I exhale.

"You. Are. Evil," I say.

He places my armband in the bag I will take to the theater and slowly shakes his hooded head.

"That is actually a common misconception," says Death.

He picks up my other armband and starts sewing again.

8.

"What?" I ask impatiently.

Death just sits there, with his arms crossed, looking at me.

"What??" I ask again.

He uncrosses his arms.

"You're doing it again," he says.

"Shut up, I am not," I say, quickly.

He waits.

"Fine," I say. "I am. Who cares?"

"Well, *you* should," he says.

Death is bossy.

"Do you?" he prods.

"What?" I ask.

"Care?" he says.

I take a deep breath in. The sigh I exhale bleeds out from where it is anchored in the bottom of my ribcage.

"Fine," I say. "I care."

The tears come hot and fast.

Death nods his head.

"I knew it," he says.

"I hate you," I say.

"Why?" he asks.

I look at him.

"Because you think you know everything," I say.

"I don't know everything," says Death, handing me a tissue.

"I only know the endings."

I blow my nose.

9.

"I get it! I get it! I get it!" I say, running into the kitchen.

Startled, Death spills chocolate chips on the floor.

He looks at me.

I narrow my eyes.

"What are you doing?" I ask.

"Nothing," he says, dusting flour off of his dark shroud.

I purse my lips.

"Well, what do you get?" he asks.

I hesitate.

"Do you, uh, need help?" I ask.

Death sighs. He looks down at his long bony fingers covered in dark draping nothingness.

"Maybe with the teaspoons," he says.

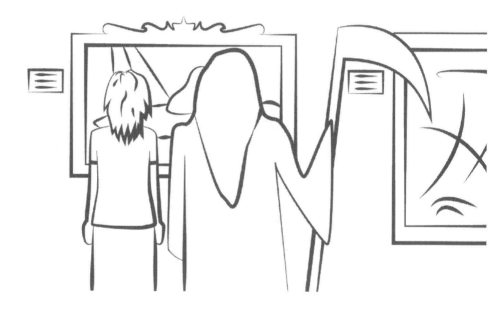

10.

A woman is speaking to the manager at the art museum.

"I'm impressed with your experimental work," she says.

"Pardon me?" asks the manager.

"I'm *impressed* with your *experimental* work!" she says, raising her voice. "It's very brave and…unexpected."

"*Pardon* me?" asks the manager, again.

"Ma'am, we do not do anything experimental at this museum," he clarifies.

"Well, I suppose you could call it an extension of Romanticism à la Fuseli," observes the woman.

"Is that what you were going for?" she asks.

"*Pardon me*?" asks the manager.

The woman narrows her eyes.

"You know," she says, "it's quite inconsiderate to be so remiss about proper signage for your work, especially when it's drawing such a crowd."

The woman leaves the museum in a huff.

At the other end of the gallery,

Death and I observe Fuseli's *The Nightmare*.

"It's not quite right, is it?" I ask,

pointing to the depiction of Death as a goblin.

Death is quiet.

"What is it?" I ask him.

"Um, maybe we should go," says Death.

"People are staring at me."

11.
A postcard arrives at my house addressed to Death.
I hand it to him.
"Look," I say. "You've got groupies."
Death takes the card.
"Well," he says. "That's a first."

12.
"Death!" I say, suddenly.
"What is it?" He does not look away from the television.
Star Wars is playing.
"I forgot to write a Death Poem today!" I say.
Death looks at me.
"You forgot what now?" he asks.
"To write a Death Poem!" I say. "And it's almost midnight!"
I scurry over to my laptop.
Death pauses the movie.
"You're…writing poems about me?" he asks.
"Yeah," I say. I type furiously.
Death is quiet. I look over at him.
"What?" I ask.
"Nothing," he says. "I just thought, you know, you'd ask my permission or something."
I pause.
"Do you *mind* that I'm writing poems about you?" I ask him.
"Well," he hesitates, "I don't know. Are they any good?"
"Um," I hesitate, "I'm not sure. I think they're funny."
Death tilts his head.
"Do you think *I'm* funny?" he asks.
"I think you're frakkin' hilarious," I say,
and I go back to writing.
Death nods his head.
"I can be mighty witty," he says to himself,
unpausing *Star Wars*.

13.
"Death!" I call from my room.
No answer.
"Deee-aaaath!!!"
Nothing.
Sigh.
I must go in search of Death, apparently.
But, I can't find him.
Not baking cookies. Not sewing costumes.
Weird.
I call my mother.
"Hi, honey," she answers.
I don't have time for small talk.
"Have you seen Death?" I ask her.
She doesn't reply for a long moment.
"Yes," she says, finally.
"He's here. I'm feeding him beef stroganoff."
"Why?" I ask.
"Well, honey," she says, slowly.
"He says that you don't need him anymore."
I think about this for a moment.
"Fine," I say. "Tell him to call me after dinner."
"Well," says my mother.
"We're actually going to see a movie after dinner."
"Oh," I say. "What are you seeing?"
"I don't know," says my mother. "Something funny.
You know how Death hates the scary ones."
"Right," I say. "Well, have fun."
I hang up the phone.
The house and I are very quiet.

14.

"Hey," I say to Death. "You're back."

"Yeah," he says. He sits at the table and sips his coffee.

I nod and put the grocery bags on the counter.

Death is silent.

I put the French vanilla soy creamer in the fridge.

I look at Death.

"You okay?" I ask.

Death sighs.

"Yeah," he replies.

I put the Japanese-style fried rice in the freezer.

I look at Death again.

"You want to talk about it?" I ask.

"No," says Death. "I don't know."

I put the grapefruit juice in the fridge and sit down at the table with Death.

"What's going on?" I ask.

Death looks at me.

"Nothing," he says, and takes another sip of coffee.

"Just feeling down today."

We look at each other.

Then, I can't help it. I burst out laughing.

"I'm sorry!" I say, giggle-tears streaming down my face.

Death is laughing, too.

"No, I know! It's funny!" he says.

"Because you're Death!" I shout.

"And you're feeling down! And you're Death!"

My cheeks hurt from smiling.

"I know!" says Death, trying to catch his breath.

Our chuckles finally die away,

and we settle into silence once again.

"So," I say. "Wanna watch 'Smash'?"

Death looks at me.

"Only if we can eat cookies," he says.

I smile.

"Deal," I say.

15.

"Hey, Jimmy. Where do you think you're going?"

Jimmy stops, straightens his shoulders, tries to look taller.

"Home, Tommy." Keeps walking.

Tommy pushes him from behind.

"Gimme some money!"

"NO!" Jimmy pushes him back with all his might.

"Oh, you're in trouble now, sucker!" yells Tommy.

Tommy grabs Jimmy's arm, twisting it until it is angry red.

Jimmy howls. But then, Tommy screams, too.

And lets go. And runs away. Fast.

Jimmy looks after him, confused.

"Yeah!" Jimmy yells. "You better run!"

Then, Jimmy turns around.

But…nothing.

Death and I are now giggling behind my garage.

"Do you feel better?" I ask.

"A little," says Death.

16.
"Do you have any relationship advice?" I ask Death.
Death looks at me.
"I'm serious," I say. Death sighs.
"You're not serious," he says.
"No, I am," I insist. "I want to know."
Death leans back and straightens his shroudy dark robes.
"Fine," he says, looking at me.
"You need to give people a break."
"Whoa. Wait a minute," I say to Death.
"You asked," he says, shrugging.
I get up from the table and grab Charlie's leash.
"Are you mad?" asks Death.
"No," I say. I call the dog. He comes running into the room
with a ball in his mouth. He looks at me. He looks at Death.
He trots over to Death and drops the ball in front of him.
"By the way," says Death, picking up the ball.
"That includes you."
He tosses the ball gently across the room. Charlie dashes.
"I need to give myself a break?" I ask.
"Definitely," says Death, picking up the ball again as Charlie
returns with it.
Toss. Dash.
"Besides," says Death. "It's not about the thing. It's never
about the thing."
Drop. Toss. Dash.
"What's it about then?" I ask.
"It's about figuring out the thing, of course," says Death.
"It's the figuring part that makes you, you know, human."
Charlie drops the ball and snuggles at Death's feet.
"That dog doesn't like anyone, you know," I say.
"Well," says Death. "I'm not just anyone."
He leans in. "Literally," Death whispers.
I roll my eyes at Death and pet the dog.

17.

"Today is a good day," I say to Death.

"Are you surprised?" asks Death,
looking up from *Slow Dance with Sasquatch.*

"No. I don't know," I say. "I'm just happy,
for no reason in particular. Is that weird?"

"No," says Death. He reaches into his cloak of darkness and
pulls out a pocket watch.

He regards it, looks at me, and then begins to wind it.

"What are you doing?" I ask.

"Setting your clock," says Death.

"Pardon me?" I say.

"Your clock," explains Death. "It's been a little off."

"Pardon me??" I say.

He winds the pocket watch steadily and then stops, nodding
with satisfaction. It disappears into his blackness again.

He picks up his book.

"You have a Tiffany watch," I state with disbelief.

"Like I could afford that," Death says,
and he goes back to reading.

18.
Death is working hard,
scribbling on paper,
head bowed in concentration.
"What are you up to, Death?" I ask.
Death looks at me.
"Everyone's writing poetry," says Death.
"I thought I'd give it a whirl."
I sneak a peak at his work.
The top of the page reads:
creepy little tiffany poems.
"That's so not right," I say.

19.
Oven preheating.
Brown sugar measuring.
Mixing bowl washing.
Eggs cracking.
Vanilla spilling over.
Death lingers in the doorway.
"Don't," I say, without turning around.
"I wasn't," says Death, handing me the chocolate chips.

20.
"You know what's coming today," I say.
"Yes," Death says.
Death just stands next to me,
holding space,
holding life.
"It's been a year," I say.
"Yes," Death says.
Death stands next to me,
a punching bag,
a handkerchief,
a rock.
"I don't understand it," I say.
"I know," Death says.
He lets the silence stretch into eternity.
I inhale deeply.
"I'm sorry," I say, finally.
"For what?" asks Death.
"For yelling. At you. Last year," I say.
"Oh," says Death. "It's okay."
I stare at the ground.
A tiny ant navigates its way into the grass.
I put my hand on my chest and press down hard,
holding it together.
"I think my heart has an echo," I say to Death.
"It feels cavernous inside of me."
"I'm not surprised you think that," says Death.
"You are kind of a hypochondriac."
I look at him.
"Shut up, Death," I say, smiling.

21.
"I'm going to vomit."
Death waits patiently,
leaning up against the door of the Whistle Stop bar,
reading the paper.
It's six in the afternoon.
"You're going to be fine," says Death
from behind the Arts section.
"No," I say, doubled over. "I'm going to VOM. IT."
"Well, do it over there, then."
Death motions vaguely to the alley behind the bar.
I look at him.
"You're not being very comforting," I say.
Death peers at me over the theatre reviews.
"If you wanted comforting," he says, "you chose to hang out
with the wrong afterlife character."
"Ha," I say, standing upright. I take a deep breath.
"Feel better?" says Death.
"No," I say.
"Be awesome," says Death.
"Aren't you coming inside?" I ask.
"Nah," says Death. "I don't want to steal your spotlight."
"Thanks, I guess," I say and head into the bar.
"Knock 'em dead!" yells Death after me.
"You're not funny!" I yell back.

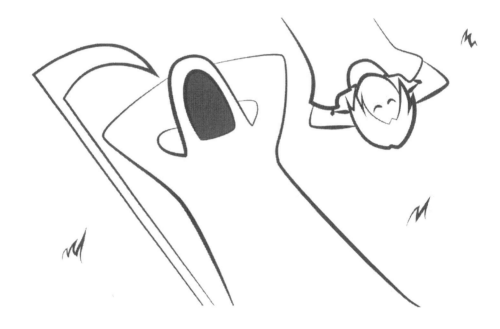

22.
"I don't see it."
"Wait for it."
…
"I don't see it."
"Wait for it!"
…
"I'm waiting."
"Be patient," I say. "Wait…there." I point to the sky.
Death and I are lying on our backs in my backyard.
He peers into the darkness,
following the trajectory of my finger.
"I don't see it," he says. "Oh, wait. Is that it?"
The tiny spot of light slowly careens across the night sky.
"That's it," I breathe, lowering my arm.
We watch the International Space Station fly by,
a shooting star, a pinhole.
"Just think about it," I say.
"All those astronauts, floating in space, watching the Earth
spin underneath them while they have breakfast."
"Tang," says Death.
"What?" I say.
"Astronauts drink Tang. For breakfast."
"That is not a true thing," I say,
"that is a made up commercial thing."
"I'm pretty sure it's true," says Death.
I sigh.
"You know you're spoiling the moment, right?"
"Tang is good," says Death. "Did you ever drink it?"
"I hate you so much right now, Death."
Death looks at me.
"Try drinking some Tang," says Death.
"It will make you feel better."

23.

Tiffany stares at her phone.
She watches the call come through, linger, and disappear.
She inhales deeply, picks up her coffee cup, holds it warm against
her chest, leans back in her chair, looks out the window.
She breathes.
Then, she turns, eyes narrowed.
She speaks –

Death is staring at me, pen poised over paper.

"Why are you being such a creeper?" I ask him.

"I forgot to write my Tiffany Poem today," says Death.

24.

"Death, you have to help me."

"What is it?"

"I -- Wait, what are you doing?"

"Nothing. Why?"

Death uses his Nicodemus robes to obscure the countertop.

"What is that?"

"What?"

"That. What are you making?"

"Oh. This?" Death steps aside,
revealing the neon orange canister.

I look at him.

"Seriously, Death?"

Death shrugs.

"What? It's good. You should try some."

Death scoops out the orange powder.

I give Death the evil eye.

Death looks at me.

"Exactly what evil do you think is going to befall *me*?"

"Good point," I say, surrendering my stare.

Death stirs his Tang.

"So…what's up?" he asks.

I shake my head.

"Nevermind, Death," I say.

25.
"Pit of despair," I say.

"Really?" says Death.

"For sure," I say. "Pit of despair, for sure."

"Hmm," says Death. "I don't believe you."

"Why not?" I say. "It's completely true."

"No," says Death. "Not so."

"I can hardly function, Death. Seriously. Pit-of-despair-gloom. No doubt about it."

"Nope."

I look at Death.

"Why are you arguing with me?"

"Because I don't believe you," says Death.

"Why not?"

"Because, Tiffany, you bought twinkle lights today."

A moment passes.

I inhale slowly.

"I did, didn't I?" I whisper.

"Yes, you did," says Death. "And I'm pretty sure the pit of despair is not decorated with twinkle lights."

A moment passes.

"I should probably hang them up," I say.

"I'll help you," Death says quickly.

26.

"Do you think I'll ever find love?" Death asks.

I stop perusing the cookie recipe book.

I look over at Death where he is lounging on the couch, twirling the edge of his robes as they fade into oblivion.

"I don't know," I say to him. "Do you, um, *want* to find love?"

Death looks at me.

"Everyone wants to find love," says Death, quietly.

"Oh," I say.

A moment passes.

"This…is a strange conversation," I observe.

I go back to my book.

Death sighs, leans over to me.

"Of all of the conversations that we have had," says Death, "you think *this* one is the strange one?"

I furrow my brow.

"I think," I say, slowly, "that if I can have 20-something conversations with Death, then anything is possible."

I close the recipe book.

"I give up," I say.

"Never give up," says Death.

I look at him.

He gives me a thumbs-up from beneath his flowy blackness.

I shake my head and re-shelve the book.

27.

"What are you doing?" Death asks.

"Planning," I say, focusing on my laptop.

"Zombie apocalypse?" asks Death.

"No," I say, typing furiously. "I'm motivating myself."

Death is quiet.

"Tomorrow is a new day," I say, typing passionately.

"Things are going to change," I say, typing madly.

"I'm inspired," I say, typing with gusto.

Death is quiet.

I type slower.

"What?" I ask.

"Nothing," says Death. "Just…how are you going to feel tomorrow when you don't do any of that stuff that you are writing about?"

I pause in my typing.

I sit still for a moment.

"Maybe tomorrow," I finally say, quietly, "will be different."

"Maybe," says Death.

We look at each other.

"Well," I say. "We could just create a zombie apocalypse Pinterest board instead."

"Okay," says Death.

28.

"You know," says Death, "writing about doing the thing is not the same as doing the thing."

I edit our Pinterest board description.

"I know," I say.

Death pins a portrait of a cabin in the woods.

"So maybe instead of writing about doing the thing, just…I don't know…do the thing. Instead," says Death.

I pin an e-card about bath salts.

"Sometimes," I say, "it feels the same."

Death pins the poster for the cult flick, *American Zombie*.

"I know," he says. "It's because you're a good writer. But it's not the same."

"I know," I say. "I just feel scared sometimes."

Death looks at our zombie apocalypse board and then at me.

I look at Death and then at our zombie apocalypse board.

"Zombies feel safer," I say, shrugging.

He nods.

"They are," says Death.

29.

"Where's Death?" my mother asks.

I look around. I spot him out back.

"He's out by the pool," I say.

"Well, see if he wants a sandwich," she says.

I wander through the sliding glass door.

Death sits with his feet dangling in the pool.

He is lost in thought, watching the sunlight dance on the clear, chlorinated water. He looks up at me as I approach.

"Mom wants to know if you want a sandwich," I say.

"No," he says quietly. "I'm good."

I sit down on the hot cement next to him
and stick my feet into the cool water.

We sit in our familiar shared silence for a moment.

Death keeps staring at the deep shimmering water.

I watch Death stare at the water.

After a moment, I ask. "Do you ever think about…?"

"Sometimes," says Death.

"But you wouldn't ever…"

"Probably not," says Death, quickly. He looks at me.

"It's a little redundant."

I look down at my feet through the water.

I swirl them around.

I knew he was going to say that.

The author wishes to thank her family for not worrying too much when she began writing death poems.

She especially wishes to thank her mother for… simply everything.

She is also profoundly grateful to all of the creepy little death poem believers out there, who suspected there was something shiny here from the very beginning.

- Paul Savage

Tiffany Tang is a writer, actor and sci-fi geek. A graduate of Mount Holyoke College, the University of Kent at Canterbury and the Actors Studio Drama School, she currently resides in her hometown of San Diego, California, where she is a contributor to the *San Diego Union-Tribune* and a writer for Intrepid Shakespeare Company. Her personal musings are at www.tiffanyanntang.com.

This is her first book.

Made in the USA
Columbia, SC
09 January 2025

49277014R00028